A Guide to Potty Training

Expert advice from:
Billie Francine Hobman, MSc, RN, RSCN, RM, RHV

Cover design by
Mary Cartwright
and Laura Hammonds

American editor:
Carrie Armstrong

US consultant:
Kimberly Wofford, MS, CDS, CCPS

A Guide to Potty Training

Caroline Young

Illustrated by Shelagh McNicholas

Design and additional illustrations by Ruth Russell

Edited by Felicity Brooks

Internet links

For further information about Usborne Parents' Guides
and to visit the websites recommended in this book, go to
www.usborne-quicklinks.com
Click on 'Parents' Guides' or type in the keywords 'potty training'.

Contents

Introduction

Most parents and caregivers are delighted to say goodbye to diapers. Even if you use super-absorbent, leak-proof, odor-controlling disposable diapers, changing them is one more job to do. You are probably looking forward to the day when your child is potty-trained; when they can take themselves to the potty or toilet and do what they need to do with little help from you.

But before you circle a start date for training on the calendar, there are several things to consider, especially how?, when? and where? As small children have minds, and bodies, very much their own, they may just not be ready to work on your schedule.

Most children crawl at around nine months and walk at around a year, but it's much harder to pinpoint when they will be potty-trained. If you accept that all children are different and that you need to adapt what you do and when you do it to suit your own child, you're much more likely to succeed. The key is to be flexible and to expect the unexpected.

Independence, for a small child, comes one step at a time, and cannot be hurried.

The training process

Potty-training is just one of the many, many things a child needs to learn as they grow up, but it is one of the things parents get most worried about. This book guides you through the whole process from start to finish. It outlines the different approaches you could take, offers advice on staying positive, and helps you to overcome any problems and setbacks you might have.

It also takes your needs into account: potty-training can be hard work, and you need to find an approach that suits your own circumstances as well as your own child. Above all, this book looks at how you can work with your child to get him or her potty-trained with the minimum mess and stress possible.

Useful tip
For the record, the average age for a child to be potty-trained (during the day) is between three and three and a half years old.

When is the right time?

Life with a small child is busy, and most people find that it's easier to cope if they plan ahead a little. We generally prefer things to happen when it suits us, and without any unexpected problems, and this could be why potty-training can come as such a shock: it doesn't fit into an ordered way of life at all. It's a process that a child has to learn – and they have to be ready to learn it before they begin.

This book describes the signs that show when your child may be ready, and takes you through all the steps to prepare for the first few diaperless days. Before this point, hard as it may be, it's important to resist the urge to make potty-training fit in with your other plans. You may want to have your child diaper-free by the end of the year, but if they show no signs of being ready to use a potty by November, you could be setting yourselves up for failure if you try to potty-train them then.

When to train

• Very few children are potty-trained before they are 30 months old and many children are still wearing a diaper at night until they are 36 months (3 years) – and some for longer.

• Before these ages, don't worry about whether your child is or isn't trained yet (no matter what family and friends may tell you).

While they are learning

Even when your child shows all the signs of being ready, they will probably still have many accidents while they are training. Learning to respond to their body's signals and managing their own toileting takes lots and lots of practice and is not something you can do for them, however much you might want to. This book shows how to deal with this tricky stage and how to stay as calm as you can while you do so.

Some children are more reluctant than others to say goodbye to diapers.

Be prepared

It may not sound very inviting, but it's a good idea to do some thinking about potty-training before you actually start. Experts agree that being well-prepared is very helpful, so this section of the book looks at some ways of getting ready to start potty-training, and helps ensure that, once you begin, you are more likely to succeed.

Before you begin

How children learn to know when they need to use the bathroom

Different approaches to potty-training, from today's experts and from earlier generations

Tips on how to stop worrying about what other people think, or what other children can do, and when

Guidance on how to handle potty-training, and what will work best for you and your child

Control of when and where to pee and poop only comes over time, as a child matures, and as you teach them.

Peeing

1. A newborn baby is totally unaware of when it needs to urinate, and of when it is going or has just gone.

2. Babies' bladders need emptying up to 20 times a day, but they don't know the pee's coming, and they can't wait.

3. As the months pass, some babies dislike being in a wet diaper, but have no idea why their diaper is suddenly soggy.

Pooping

1. As all parents and caregivers know, babies fill their diapers whenever they need to without knowing or caring that you've just changed it.

2. For at least a year, babies will fill their diapers several times a day, but have absolutely no awareness of having done so.

3. Gradually, a child usually begins to show you that they are about to poop, perhaps by grunting, straining, or a red face.

Ages and stages

It's probably fair to say that most people don't spend much time thinking about how they know whether they need to go to the bathroom. (For the record, the relevant parts of our bodies send 'signals' to our brains that tell us.) For a child, however, learning to understand these bodily signals is as much of a learning curve as anything else they have to do.

When and where

The main stages a young baby goes through when learning to understand bodily signals are listed on the left of this page. Most babies realize when they have a dirty diaper before they notice a wet one, but this can vary a great deal. Some children remain completely oblivious of the contents of their diaper for much longer than others.

If you want to find out more, there's information about how our bodies work, and how specific muscles interact with our brains to prompt us to use the bathroom at the Usborne Quicklinks Website (see page 61).

For many months babies do what they need to do in a diaper without even knowing about it.

In their own time

Some children so dislike a wet or dirty diaper that they do learn faster than others to use a potty, or toilet. Others will happily sit in a smelly diaper for hours, if you let them. Every child is different, and will learn what's expected of them in their own time, with your support. The process is gradual, but it does happen in several clearly-defined stages, over time. To help you know what to look for, there's a chart that shows roughly what to expect a child to be able to do, and when, on pages 55 to 57 of this book.

Experts have found that boys are often slower to respond to their bodies' messages about toileting than girls. This book has extra information, and tips for training little boys, wherever it is relevant and may help you.

Useful tip
It helps babies to become aware of what their bodies are producing if you tell them what you find in their diapers (see also page 16).

Help me learn

Your main goal is to help small children begin to understand their bodies' signals, and this will take time, and patience. Of course, it can be irritating when a just-changed baby poops all over the changing pad or a little boy tinkles on you before you can get another diaper on him, but remember that, for them, going to the bathroom is anything but private, or controllable. Bladder control and the idea of privacy are just two more of the many things they have to learn.

Some older babies are fascinated with what goes on in their diapers.

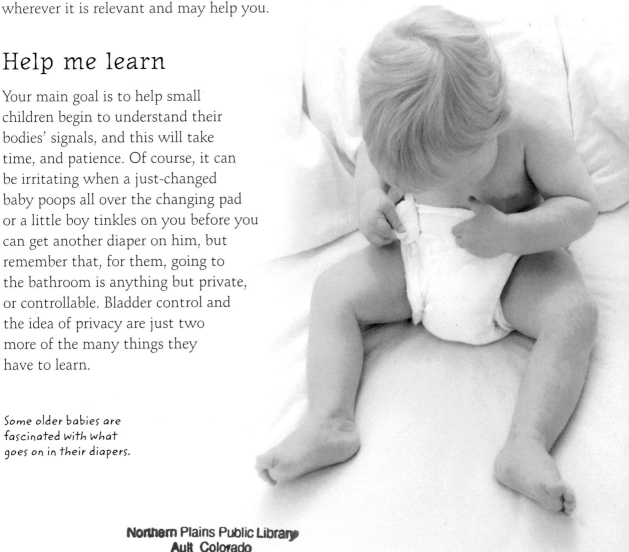

It's your choice

Once you start thinking about potty-training your child, you may start searching out books and websites with expert advice on the best way of doing it. It can be a minefield of different opinions and tactics, all of which make it harder for you to know what to do. These pages look at four different approaches to potty-training.

Starting early

In the days before washing machines and disposables, people tended to potty-train early – sometimes when babies were only a few months old. The idea of dangling a tiny baby over a potty may seem strange to us today, but this method is still used exclusively in some parts of the world. There are people who favor potty training earlier than 18 months, but this method has big disadvantages.

A baby below this age won't really understand what's happening, won't be able to dress and undress themselves and will have little control over when they pee or poop. Before a baby has control of their bladder and bowels, it is the parent who is 'trained', not the child.

In some parts of the world early potty training is a necessity. (A baby can go through at least 5,000 diapers before being toilet-trained.)

Tell me when you're ready

Some people argue that you should wait for your child to let you know when they are ready to come out of diapers. This method has the advantage of giving you some stress-free months when others around you may be knee-deep in soggy pants, and perhaps keeping some children happier in some ways, but there are downsides.

Most children naturally arrive at the point where they are ready to be potty-trained. The signs to look for are listed on pages 20 to 21. Others need a little more coaxing, and for some parents it can feel risky handing over control of the potty training process. There is much to recommend this method, but it can cause problems, too.

Sometimes, a child will let you know when they are ready to start being potty-trained.

Intensive training

Parents and caregivers are always busy, so the idea of intensive potty-training, or choosing a day to take diapers off and staying inside until a child successfully uses the potty, is very appealing. A child still needs to be physically and emotionally ready to embark on this process, so it's best to avoid such quick fixes unless you are fairly sure that this is the case. Training a child intensively may limit the days of accidents and cleaning up, but as children are all different, there's unlikely to be a miraculous intensive program that will work successfully for every child.

See how it goes

This is the approach most parents and caregivers adopt, and the one this book suggests. It fits in most easily with normal life, and allows you to go out when you need to. It involves gradually preparing a child to come out of diapers, trying them on a potty, cleaning up lots of accidents and, probably, still using diapers when you go out. Its advantages are that neither the adult nor the child is under enormous pressure, but it can take time for a child to get the message.

Useful tip
You'll find more detail about different approaches to potty-training, and what steps you need to follow for each one, on pages 58 to 59.

Whichever way you choose to handle training, it's something you and your child do together.

11

Comparing your child's progress to other children's is natural, but remember that no two children are exactly the same and it's not a competition.

Children need to be willing and ready to use the potty. You can't force them to do so.

You decide

Unfortunately, it can be very easy to get uptight about potty-training. You may find that you really mind if a friend's child is out of diapers before yours, or a relative makes you feel you're a failure if there's still a package of diapers in your home. This page has some tactics to help you resist the pressures of potty-training.

Hurry up

If they are honest, most parents and caregivers worry that their child will lag behind others in their development. They wait eagerly for that first word, or first step, and are relieved when they come. They are even happier if their child's progress is roughly the same as other children of a similar age. Toilet-training is as much a part of a child's developmental progress as anything else, but problems getting a child out of diapers can make parents and caregivers feel inadequate. They may start to wonder if they should try to force a child to perform on a potty, though they would never dream of forcing a child to crawl, or walk, before they seemed ready.

Children come first

The unavoidable fact is that a child has to be ready to start potty-training. Most also need lots of encouragement, and, simply, to be trained. If they are not ready, you'll probably confuse, annoy and bore them. You may actually delay toilet-training success and could even traumatize them, by pushing it on them too soon.

It can be hard to be calm if you are surrounded by parents of diaper-free toddlers, or people who feel they have a right to tell you how to do things. You may feel a sense of failure when someone makes a comment about your child still wearing a diaper, for instance. Remember that your child's needs, and happiness, are more important than what anyone else thinks, or any other child does.

Getting ready

Now that you know a little more about some
of the possible pitfalls of potty-training, and how
to survive them, this part of the book has some
practical suggestions to help you both get ready to
begin. They will help to ensure a smooth transition
from diaper to potty, and should help a child
understand a lot more about what's going to happen.

Help and advice

How and when to introduce a child to potties

What kind of potty to buy and how many

Useful tips for keeping a child relaxed
about their toileting needs

Advice on what words to use to talk
about toileting

Signs that show when a child is ready
to be potty-trained

The potty needs to become just another part of everyday life for your child.

Potty pals

The main piece of equipment you need to potty-train your child is, of course, a potty chair. In fact, it's a good idea to get one before you even begin training, so that it's familiar, and not new or scary, when it's time for your child to use it as you want them to. Here are some suggestions to help make your child more comfortable with the whole idea of using a potty.

Which potty?

Unfortunately, buying a potty chair is not as simple as it sounds. There's now such a huge range available, that it can be hard to know which one to choose. Manufacturers make potties that play a tune, light up, look like chairs, or are shaped like dogs or frogs, but none of them guarantees any more success than the most basic design. (In fact, it's probably not a good idea to encourage your child to go to the toilet on something that looks like a chair, anyway.) As a general rule, a potty is a means to an end, and, hopefully, won't be used for very long. Avoid spending a lot of money on one unless you are really convinced it will entice your child to use it more readily. On the left are four potty chair design essentials to bear in mind.

Potty chair design

• *Make sure that the potty is light, but sturdy.*

• *A hole, or handle, makes carrying easier.*

• *If it's a bright color, it may be more appealing.*

• *A raised lip will help stop urine from splashing out.*

Talk to your child about how the arrival of a potty in the house means that they are becoming a big boy or girl.

Introducing the potty

Some experts argue that the more potties you have around your home, the more likely your child is, eventually, to use one. It seems sensible to make sure you put a potty in the bathroom, near the toilet. If you want to put a potty in other rooms, it may mean less sprinting to get one later on, but will also mean that no part of your home will be a potty-free zone for a while.

When you introduce the potty, tell your child what it is, and that they will, one day, pee and poop in it. If they seem interested, let them sit on it whenever they want to, either in or out of a diaper. Your goal is to make them comfortable with their potty and the idea of sitting on it, so allow them some freedom to get to know it. For them, the whole business can be quite exciting, which is something for you to encourage.

Children often enjoy the novelty of sitting on their potty, though they may not use it for a while.

Potty care

It is important to keep potties clean, even before they are used properly. Don't let children put a potty near their mouth, or put food in it. The message to get across from the very beginning is that potties are where big boys and girls pee and poop. The potties may become familiar objects after a while, which is good, but they do have a particular function. Make sure your child is always aware that potties are not for playing with, and try to keep high standards of potty hygiene.

Potty-training will be a lot easier if you accept that potties, and toilets, will play a central role in both your lives.

Toilet talk

Not everybody feels comfortable talking about what goes on in the toilet, but as the parent or caregiver of a small child, you may well find that you have to be. Talking about pee, poop, diapers, potties and toilets openly from their baby days onward helps a child prepare for potty training. Remembering this might help you abandon grown-up sensibilities for a while and just be prepared to talk about toilets a great deal.

What's in your diaper?

It may sound strange, but it's a good idea to make babies aware of what they've done in their diapers. There's no need to make an announcement, but talking about, and even showing them, what they have produced can help prevent a child from being shocked when they see it later on, in the bottom of a potty.

Most people use phrases such as 'You've gone poo-poo' completely naturally as they change a child's diaper. However, saying anything negative, or showing real distaste for what you find in a diaper, can make babies feel ashamed, confused or scared. This could make potty-training much harder for both of you, later on.

As you change your child's diapers, chat about what's in them in a positive, reassuring tone.

Everybody does it

Try to get everyone important in a child's life involved in talking as naturally as possible about going to the toilet. Keep it part of everyday life, rather than putting too much emphasis on it. There are some tips to help you on the right.

Two's company

Children copy what they see happening around them. Just as they mimic household tasks, such as sweeping and emptying shopping bags, so they watch and learn from what you do in the bathroom – whether you want them as your audience or not. Once a baby can crawl, most parents have to get used to having company every time they go to the bathroom. If you long for privacy at such times, take comfort from the fact that it's helpful for your child to be involved in your trips to the bathroom and that they learn from them. Forget modesty: tell your child when you need to use the bathroom, let them come too, and show them how things are done when you get there.

Some experts go further, suggesting that you give a running commentary on what you do in the bathroom; the best advice is probably to do what feels natural for you. Your goal is to get babies used to the fact that people go somewhere special to pee and poop and that the whole business is entirely normal.

For a crawling baby, nowhere you go is private. They want to be where you are.

Show me how

• *Encourage older siblings to let toddlers go with them to the bathroom. The urge to copy what older children do is a strong learning incentive.*

• *Little friends who are further along in their potty-training might enjoy showing your child what they do on their potty or in the toilet.*

• *Fathers and big brothers can help little boys a lot. Even a baby in diapers will learn from watching Dad peeing while standing up.*

• *Some dolls pee out water when fed with a bottle. These might seem gimmicky, but if they help a child get the message, that's fine.*

Useful tip

Most small children need little encouragement to talk about pee and poop. Within limits, just let them.

'Pee', 'pee-pee' or 'number one'?

Encouraging a child to be comfortable talking about what their body produces, either in a diaper or potty, is all very positive, but it's a good idea to set some limits in this area, too. This page gives you some ideas for setting a few ground rules, so that children begin to learn what is acceptable for them to say and do, and what is not.

Which words?

Small children have little idea which words are polite, and which are rude. If you are thinking about potty-training a child, you need to decide what you are going to call the key things you'll need to talk about. Your child will copy the words you choose, so choose with care. Remember that you'll need words for urine, feces, the vagina, the anus, the penis and for passing gas. You'll need words that you're happy to use in public, as your child is unlikely to wait for a quiet moment to say them to you discreetly. Lastly, you must be prepared to hear these words often, as they may fascinate a child for quite some time.

Some people prefer to use more child-friendly words, such as 'pee-pee' and 'poo-poo'. Others prefer 'number one' or 'number two', and some choose the, reasonably bland, 'pee' and 'poop', which this book uses. There are families who choose to use the proper names, such as vagina and penis, for body parts. As long as everyone in your child's life uses the same words, without embarrassment, there should be no problems.

Useful tip

The toilet words you choose are up to you, but try picturing you and your child in a busy supermarket when you make that choice.

Children should not be made to feel self-conscious about peeing and pooping.

Ssshhh...!

However you describe going to the bathroom, it's worth emphasizing that young children do not share your ideas of politeness, or discretion. If they need to go to the bathroom, or have just been, they will tell you – probably loudly.

It's best to accept right at the start that good manners are something we all learn over time. Try not to be embarrassed with a child who announces to everybody on the bus that he has just pooped. Remember that everyone was a small child once, so few people are likely to be offended.

For a child, their needs are always urgent. They haven't yet learned to wait for a good time to tell you about them.

Potties are everywhere

Talking about potties, pee and poop is always interesting for a child, but probably less so for you. Luckily, there are lots of good children's books and DVDs to help you vary the way you tackle the subject. They can make it more friendly and familiar, as they often have simple stories about children using potties in the 'wrong' way and doing silly things with them.

Useful tip

It's important to keep your child interested, and motivated to succeed in using their potty properly.

These funny potty stories are a great way of making clear to young children what is appropriate (sitting on the potty), and what is not (putting the potty on your head). Phrases such as 'You don't do that with *your* potty, do you?' help them understand what they should, and shouldn't, do with a potty. It gives them a sense of being big, and responsible, too. You'll find some suggestions for potty-based stories and other resources on the Usborne Quicklinks website (see page 61).

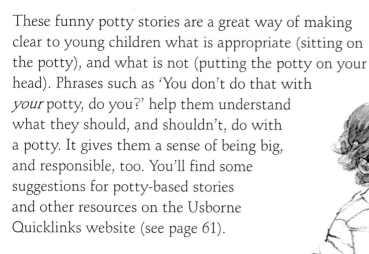

Books about potties show children that they are not the only ones using them.

Are you ready?

It can be difficult to pinpoint the ideal time to do more than just let a child become familiar with potties, and to start potty-training for real. Every child is different, but there are some signs you can look for to help you make an intelligent guess as to when to begin. Picking a time that suits you both is important (though it can be easier said than done). The following pages look at times when you may be ready to start and also at times when it's probably better to avoid trying to potty-train your child.

There can be no fail-safe checklist to mark off that will ensure that your child is ready to come out of diapers, but you may notice, over a period of several months, some of the signs that are listed on the left.

Ready to try?

• Is your child able to follow simple instructions you give them, such as 'go and get your shoes, please' ?

• Are your child's diapers dry for longer periods of time? This can mean that they are gaining more bladder control.

• Do they tell you that they've peed or pooped? Some babies don't like being in dirty diapers, and pull them off.

• Is your child starting to let you know when they need to pee or poop? If so, training them should be even easier.

• Are they interested in what goes on in the bathroom, and interested in sitting on the potty or toilet themselves?

You can often tell when a child is filling their diaper from the expression on their face, or noises they may make (as well as the smell!).

Even though there are signs that a child may be physically and emotionally ready to start potty-training, very few children display all of them at the same time. Boys, in particular, tend to mature later in several ways, and may be slower to reach each stage.

Trial run

If your child is doing some of the things listed on the previous page, it might be a good idea to let them have a short time each day, say an hour or so, without a diaper on. Choose a similar time, perhaps after a meal, show them their potty, and tell them that's where they need to pee and poop. Don't be surprised, or upset, if they forget to use it at all, however. This tells you that it's best to wait a little longer before starting training.

During these months, when children seem almost ready to try without diapers, many people decide to put them in disposable trainer pants. These are elastic diapers that can be pulled up and down like pants. It's not a good idea to use them at this stage, as most children treat them as they do a diaper, and freely pee and poop in them. See page 32 for when you might choose to use training pants.

Diaper-free time

If you happen to be potty training when the weather is warm, you could let your child play outside without a diaper or clothes on. You could also put a potty outside so your child can practice sitting on the potty without clothes getting in the way. There would also be less mess to clean up if there are accidents.

Most toddlers are more than happy to spend some time without their clothes on, whether they are in diapers or not.

Think twice

For most children, potty-training involves a big change in their lives. You are asking them to learn quite a few new things, all at the same time. Sometimes, however anxious you are to get your child out of diapers, it can be more sensible to wait before starting potty-training. The main reasons for holding off a while are listed on the left. This page helps you decide if waiting might be best for you and your child.

Why wait?

Taking care of small children is hard work, and potty-training adds to that. For a child to be successful in learning how to use the potty, the whole experience should be as positive as possible. If you feel that there are reasons why you might not be able to ensure that this is the case, wait a while. It will be best for both of you.

Reasons to wait

• Wait if you are especially tired, stressed, or have a very busy period ahead at work.

• If you are pregnant, or have just had a baby, you might feel stronger in a few weeks.

• Wait if you are planning a vacation, or to visit a potty-less, cream-carpeted house soon.

• If your child's behavior is difficult at present, wait until they are in a calmer phase.

• Wait if your child seems unwilling to try training, or to be without their diaper on.

Small things can affect the training process a great deal. Starting on a Friday might mean you have more help over the weekend, for instance. Your mood, and energy levels, can have a big impact on things as well.

If a new baby has recently arrived, it may be easier to wait to train your toddler.

Training can wait

If, for any reason, you really feel that cleaning up after your child might just be the last straw right now, it's better to postpone potty-training. Unlike a newborn baby needing a night feeding, potty-training can wait for a few weeks without anybody coming to any harm.

Taking the plunge

By now, you've bought the potty, encouraged your child to sit on it, talked endlessly about pee and poop, and let them enjoy some diaper-free time. The next part of the book looks at the days you decide to say goodbye to diapers during the day and start training for real. This stage will be easy for some people; others find it more difficult. Remember there is a useful potty-training chart to refer to on pages 55 to 57 of this book.

Before you begin

Guidance on what to do on the first few days
your child is without diapers

Lots of tips on how to keep going when things
get tough, or you get fed-up

Advice on how to encourage a child who
is finding training hard

Tips on how to handle going out
with a nearly-trained child

Most small children will be excited at the prospect of wearing their very own underwear.

Getting ready

It's up to you to help make these first few diaperless days as positive as possible. Here are four tips to help.

1. Before you begin, make sure you have plenty of old, comfy clothes ready for your child to wear.

2. Tell your child that they are going to wear big boy's/ girl's underwear from today on, and how proud you are of them.

3. Put their potty, or potties, where you want them to be. Show them to your child and tell them what's expected.

4. To minimize stress, be ready for accidents and have cleaning supplies ready.

The first diaper-free days

Everything that you and your child have done so far to get them used to the idea of using the potty is in preparation for the day when you decide to take your child out of diapers during the day. This is a big step for them, and perhaps for you, too. These pages guide you through that very first diaperless day.

Choosing underwear

Of course, before you actually take off your child's diapers, you need to make sure you've bought them some underwear to wear instead. Most children will enjoy choosing their own, and doing so can make them reluctant to get them wet or dirty. It certainly makes a happy final step in their pre-potty-training preparations.

Let your child see, and feel, the differences between diapers and underwear.

Watch and wait

The next step, after dressing your child in their new underwear and suitable clothing, is to watch and wait. It's a good idea to prompt them to sit on the potty reasonably frequently, but don't interrupt their play to ask if they need to do so too often. This may just make them resentful and bored.

Remember that you're aiming for your child to understand and respond to their body's signals themselves, so avoid intervening too much at this early stage. You will, of course, have their toileting needs very much in mind during the day, but try not to let this take over. Make sure you both have some happy, potty-free time too.

Children often learn from what they see others doing.

Accidents happen

There are bound to be accidents. A few children come out of diapers and start peeing and pooping in a potty right away, but the vast majority need time to learn to interpret, and control, what their body needs to do.

You may be lucky, and catch most of the pees and poops a child does in the potty, but if not, don't make them sit on a potty until they do something. They will just get fed-up and be less willing to sit on it again. You can encourage reluctant potty-sitters to stay on it for a little longer by reading them a favorite book, but a few minutes is probably the longest they should sit there.

Plan to handle any accidents the day brings calmly. Clean up with hot, soapy water, and put any wet clothes straight into the washing machine (rinsing dirty ones off first), to wait for your next load. If it's a warm day, you could let a child play in just their underwear to reduce extra washing.

Useful tip
For daytime naps, put your child in diapers or put some padding, such as towels, under them.

Cleaning up puddles is not much fun, but this stage of training won't last forever.

Keeping going

Your child may have gotten through one whole day without a diaper, but it can be hard to face more accidents and clothes-washing on the days that follow. It's best to accept at the outset that, for most children, the training process is gradual, and takes time. Here are some ideas to help iron out some common early setbacks, and help you keep going.

Useful tip

When you need to leave the house during these early stages, see pages 32 and 33 for tips.

Gentle reminders

Remember that your attitude to training makes a big difference. Praise your child every time they manage to tell you that they need the potty, and do something in it. Don't go too over the top, however – just let them know that you are pleased with them.

One of the main mistakes people make if a child is regularly not getting to the potty in time is to remind them to sit on it more often. This is natural, but can be counter-productive. Some children stop trying to make it to the potty themselves, and others say they need it just to see you jump up to get it.

Keeping your cool

It's important to try to be consistent in your approach (which can be hard as you become steadily more frazzled). Try to establish some very basic potty-routines in your household, and try to stick to them.

It's a good idea to bear in mind that, in most cases, children want to please the people who care for them. Many become so worried about their parents getting upset if they don't make it to the potty in time that they'll ask them for it without really needing it – which will make you upset anyway! It's important to see things from your child's point of view as much as you can.

It's fine if children want to help you clean up, but don't make it seem like a punishment.

Say how you feel

It's easy to feel tired and frustrated if your child is creating extra work for you. It's also acceptable to gently tell them so, as long as you use phrases that won't scare them, such as 'I'm tired, Sam. Next time, try doing it in the potty.'

If you do lose your temper at the umpteenth puddle on the floor that morning, don't feel guilty. Nobody has endless patience, however good their intentions.
Say sorry with a hug, start again and remember that few children have accidents deliberately.

There's bound to be more laundry during potty-training, but it won't always be like this.

Potty-training is a learning curve for both of you, so don't expect too much of yourselves.

Keep calm

• Count slowly to ten before saying anything when you find the latest puddle or pile.

• Have a phrase you always say, such as 'It's OK. It was an accident,' for example.

• Take a really long, deep breath before going to get things to clean up the mess.

• If you are really worn out, can someone else do potty duty for a while?

Step back

Children can quickly switch off if they are confused about what they are supposed to do. Sometimes, a child starts off well, but then gets involved in other, more exciting, things, and forgets all about sitting on the potty. If this is happening to you and your child, or you are getting very stressed about their continuing accidents, step back and try the tactics on the right to help you keep calm.

Survival tactics

If all goes well for a few days, and the successes outnumber the accidents, you'll probably be feeling pretty good about deciding to try potty-training your child. If this is the case, you are lucky. For many people, things don't go this smoothly. On these pages, you'll find some tactics to try if you've hit a tricky phase, and are feeling thoroughly fed-up with potty-training.

Rewards

If things are not going well, and the days are passing without much progress, the ideas on the left might help you see things in a more positive light. To encourage your child, think about whether offering a small 'prize' for each successful trip to the potty might help motivate them.

Avoid making a trip to sit on the potty a punishment. You need your child to stay willing.

Don't despair

• Think about whether your child is actually having that many accidents. Keep track of exactly what goes on in a day. You may find things are not as bad as you had thought, and feel a little better.

• If you are surrounded by potty-trained toddlers, it's easy to feel that you and your child have failed. Stay positive, and keep reminding yourself that different children have different needs.

• Talk to other people, who have been through this. Did they have similarly shaky times? Feeling that you're not the only one may be all you need to encourage you to keep at it.

You could draw up a 'star chart', and explain to your child that every pee or poop in the potty will earn them a star, with perhaps every six stars earning them a small reward. What that reward may be is often less important to the child than the fact that they could win it. Simple treats, such as letting them pour lots of bubbles into their bath, often work well.

Remember not to get upset if your child still can't manage to make it to the potty. They will have wanted to get those stars, and that reward, just as much as you wanted them to. Make light of it, and keep encouraging them.

If you use a star chart, explain how the stars add up.

Problem-solving

It can be hard to analyze exactly what's going wrong when you're in the middle of it all. Below are three common problems that are easily solved.

• If a boy regularly misses the potty, check the lip is at the front of the potty. Is his penis pointing downward, so that pee flows into the potty?

• If a child regularly has accidents in a particular place or room, can you put a potty there? You can move it later but it might help now.

• If a child regularly pees or poops after a meal, make sure they always sit on the potty then. Each success they have will encourage you both.

Keeping a potty close by often jogs a child's memory to use it.

Trust yourself

Problem-solving tactics are all very well, but you do need to trust yourself. However determined you are to master potty-training, you can't force a child to use the potty. You may need to rethink after a while if things are becoming very stressful and accidents are still outnumbering successes by a long way. It's better to try again in a few weeks, or months, than make your child miserable. Perhaps they were not quite ready after all, and children learn things in their own good time, and not necessarily when you want them to. Pushing them when they're unwilling or unable to do something is utterly pointless and will make you both unhappy.

Useful tip
It can help to keep remembering that just about everyone gets there in the end and very few children start school in diapers.

Keeping a trusting, happy relationship with your child is more important than anything else.

Getting there

If a child is ready to be potty-trained, they usually understand what to do fairly quickly – often within the first few days. Gradually, the number of accidents lessens, and the number of pees and poops in the potty increases. These pages look at the next stage of training, as the potty becomes part of daily life.

Over to them

If you feel that your child is coping well, you can start to remind them to sit on the potty less often. As they develop more control over their bladder and bowels, they should start to find the potty themselves when they need it. If your child tends to need to pee as soon as they have told you they do, keep reminding them about the potty fairly regularly, however, as not getting there in time might discourage them.

You will have to supervise wiping a child's bottom for quite a while, especially if they are at the younger end of the potty-training age range. You'll also almost certainly have to supervise hand-washing too, and may still have to help out with underwear, tights or jeans. There's more about teaching children these extra toileting skills on pages 38 and 39 of this book.

Keep dressing your child in clothes that are easy for them to pull down...

... and up again.

Useful tip

Don't remind your child to use the potty more than once every 15 minutes.

Over time, most children gain more and more independence in using the potty.

Spread the news

Most children are extremely proud of themselves every time they do something in the potty. If you praise them, and let them help you empty the potty and flush the contents away, they will be even more so. A few children don't tell people when they have gone, so their potties will need regular checking. Usually, however, children announce their toileting achievements with gusto.

It's a good idea to let your child tell other people in their lives that they now use the potty. It can really increase their self-esteem and help them see how positive their behavior is. They could telephone a grandparent or a friend to tell them how well they are doing, for instance.

If your child tells you all about what they have done in the potty, listen, and congratulate them. For them, it's very important.

Among the successes, there are bound to be accidents. Many children still have them months after they last wore a diaper. Don't make a big deal about such slips, or draw attention to what's happened in front of others. Deal with the situation calmly, and show your child that you know that their accident was just that – an accident.

False start

Some children have a faultless first few days of potty-training, then have a period of time with lots of accidents. This can be a sign either that they are not quite mature enough to understand what they need to do, or that they can't yet remember to do it in time, every time. Whatever the reason, it's very frustrating.

If your child follows this pattern, and things don't improve again soon, you may need to take a step or two back in the training process. Give them some time in, and out, of diapers, and see how things go for a while before trying training again. They will get there, in their own time.

Stand or sit?

Little boys often want to stand to pee like Daddy does. Unless your child is really reluctant to use a potty, it's probably best to wait until they have some degree of control over where they pee before letting them do it standing up.

Going out

Even if you opt to stay at home for the first few days your child is out of diapers, you will eventually need to venture out. These pages help you make sure that going out with a partly-trained child is as easy as it can be.

Two choices

For most parents, not going out at all for several days is simply not an option. They may have to make local trips, such as to pick up another child from school or get something essential at the grocery store. If these circumstances apply to you, you have two main choices about how to handle these unavoidable, short outings with your nearly-trained child: you can either put them in a diaper or training pants, or take a risk, and take them out in just their clothes. To help you choose, the pros and cons of both options are shown on the left.

Many toddlers cope better than you might expect without a diaper on.

Diaper or not?

• If you decide to put your child back into a diaper or training pants, you may confuse them. This is convenient, but not very consistent, so don't choose this option on a regular basis.

• If you decide to take a risk, tell your child that you're going out and sit them on the potty. Tell them to try to pee now, but don't make them stay there too long.

Useful tip

Just before you go anywhere, encourage your child to sit on the potty and try to 'go'.

Be prepared

When you're ready for longer outings with a nearly-trained child, you need to be prepared. It's best not to put your child in training pants to go out for long: most children use them just like diapers, which is a backward step in their training. In a toileting emergency you could try putting training pants on top of underwear.

Think about where you're going: this may not be the time to visit a childless friend with an immaculate house. Wherever you're going together, remember that the worst thing that could happen is that your child soaks, or dirties, their clothes, their stroller and/or car seat, and perhaps even your lap. On the right are some ways of dealing with these things, if they happen.

Preparation checklist

* *Take at least one change of dry clothing for your child with you (including socks).*

* *Take bags and wipes, and if you are staying overnight somewhere take a potty with you.*

* *Cover strollers or car seats with towels, unfolded diapers or taped-down plastic bags.*

* *If getting a damp lap would cause real problems, take dry clothes for yourself too.*

Little and often

Dealing with a damp, distressed small child in public is not easy. Give your child lots of opportunities to use the restroom: frequent trips are far better than a wet floor. For a while, you may have to accept less ambitious trips out, and make frequent potty-stops along the way.

You'll still need to take a diaper bag whenever you go out for a while, but it will contain dry clothes, not diapers.

If outings prove really difficult, remember that this phase will not last forever. Once children are happy to use a toilet, things get easier, as the next section of this book will show you. Before then, be reassured that your child will learn to control their toileting needs, but that the only way for them to do so is to keep practicing. It's important for both of you to get out and about regularly while you are potty-training.

Public restrooms

• Use toilet seat covers if available or carefully hold your child over a toilet.

• All restaurants should have toilets. Most stores do, too, for their staff. Ask if you can use them.

• Make sure that you both wash your hands thoroughly after using the bathroom.

Useful tip

It's a good idea to have some anti-bacterial wipes or evaporating hand-cleaning gel with you at all times.

'I need to go potty!'

These words can strike panic into most parents, but even more so if your child is in the middle of potty-training. When your child needs to go, you'll need to respond to their request quickly, as they probably can't wait long. On the left are three tips for coping with visits to public restrooms, and there's more guidance below.

However inconvenient it may be, it's important not to let a small child become anxious about the timing of their bodily functions. Trying to hold it, or worrying about having an accident, can lead to serious, longer-term problems.

If a child says they need to go, they usually mean it. Explain that there isn't a potty for them to use, but that you are going to help them use the toilet. You may have to hold them over it, but it's good to get them used to this early on. Not all public toilets are as clean as you might wish, but, with small children, you may not have a choice.

If there's a line for the toilet, explain your child's situation. Most people will let them go first.

It's private

Going to the bathroom is a private thing, and it's important to teach children this. If a young child is desperate to go, however, and the only option (other than wet pants) is to hold them over a drain or at the roadside while they do so, it's best simply to explain what has to happen, and help them – as discreetly as you can. This is not ideal, but it's just part of life with a small child. It's far better than causing them any anxiety or discomfort.

Time for the toilet

There is no right time for a child to start using the toilet. Most use a potty before they do so, others skip potties and go straight to the toilet. A few use both potties and toilets. This part of the book looks at how to introduce a child to using a toilet, whenever you decide to do it.

A step up

Advice on how to make sure a child is happy about starting to use the toilet

Information about equipment that will make it easier for your child to use the toilet independently

How to establish a 'toilet routine', including hand-washing and bottom-wiping

Tips and techniques to help little boys use the toilet successfully

For a small child, there's a
lot to remember to do each
time they use the bathroom.

Disadvantages

• There may not be a toilet
nearby exactly when your
child needs one. They may
have to learn to wait.

• Many public toilets are
dirty, and not at all child-
friendly. Find out the best
ones in your area.

• Your own toilet will need
to be extra clean for a
while as your child will be
touching it often.

• Some children are scared
of the flush, or of falling
into the toilet. There are
tips to help on page 37.

Using the toilet

For some children, making the transition from
the potty to the toilet is easy; for others it takes
longer. These pages offer some guidelines
to help get your child on the path
toward being able to use the
toilet independently.

*Children often feel
happier sitting on a
child-sized toilet
training seat.*

Pros and cons

If your child seems ready and willing, give them the chance
to try using a toilet. Some small children prefer to sit on
the toilet rather than a potty from the beginning, but you'll
need to make sure they feel secure on the toilet seat by
either holding them or providing a step stool. Just as when
children start using potties, there may be accidents during
the early days. A child may not sit back far enough on the
toilet seat, or may just not get their pants down in time.

There are many advantages when children begin using the
toilet, but there are some disadvantages too (listed on the
left). Overall, once your child can use a toilet, things are
much easier. You won't have potties dotted around your
house. You won't need to empty full potties anymore, either,
and flushing the toilet is much less of a chore. Remember
that when your child can manage their own toileting needs,
your job will be done.

Watch and learn

Your child will probably have seen you use the toilet countless times, but it's still a good idea to take the time to make sure they are comfortable about sitting on a toilet themselves before expecting them to do so regularly. You could start by putting their potty next to the toilet, and encouraging them to use it from time to time when you are using the toilet. It may sound strange, but it may really help your child feel relaxed. Let them flush for you, or pass you some toilet paper when you need it. It's all valuable learning for them. If they seem willing, let them sit on the toilet occasionally (with diapers on at first if it makes them feel more secure). Tell them how everything is washed away by all the water when you flush the toilet.

Small children tend to use too much toilet paper, so keep a close eye.

Toilet problems

Sometimes children are frightened of sitting on the toilet, or the noise or splashing of the flush. There are some ways to tackle these fears listed on the right, but if nothing helps, it may be wiser to leave toilet-training for now. This phase is nothing to worry about and usually passes quickly.

Some children like watching the toilet flush and you need to be extra vigilant about toilet hygiene if they hold onto the bowl or seat.

Toilet fears

• Don't flush until your child is off the toilet seat. If they are nervous of the flush, wait until they are out of the room.

• Put sheets of toilet paper inside the toilet bowl to reduce upward splashes.

• Hold your child while they are sitting on the toilet, or provide a step stool so that they feel secure.

Steps and seats

• Plastic steps like this one can help small children reach the toilet and sink.

• Training seats make sitting on a toilet much easier.

Children copy what they see, and want to do things just like everyone else does.

More toilet tips

Once your child has gotten used to sitting on the toilet, the ideas on these pages should help them learn to use it independently. Remember to keep things as low-key as possible, to help them feel happy and confident about being in charge of their own toileting needs. That's the main goal of all this training, after all.

Most toilets are designed for adults. They are too high for small children to get on and off easily on their own. The seats are bigger than their bottoms, too, which can make them feel that they might fall into the toilet bowl. Two inexpensive pieces of equipment solve both these problems. A plastic step helps children reach the toilet, and a plastic toilet training seat (which slots on top of the full-sized seat) fits a child's bottom and makes them feel safer.

Start to finish

Once a child can pee and poop in a toilet, they need to be able to do three more things: wipe their bottoms, flush the toilet and wash their hands. This will all take practice, and you will probably have to help them for some time to come, but try to teach them this routine from the outset. These skills will be important for the rest of their lives.

Show your child how much toilet paper to use, and how to make a pad to wipe their bottoms. Toilet wipes are useful, but you need to teach children how to use paper, too, for when wipes are not available. It's more hygienic for both girls and boys to wipe their bottoms from the front to the back. Boys should gently shake their penis over the toilet.

Washing hands and drying them well after using the toilet is essential basic hygiene, and cuts the risk of catching any illnesses spread by bacteria on or around the toilet. Children need to learn to wash their hands every time they have used the toilet.

About hand-washing

Children need to be taught about the importance of hand-washing and hygiene from an early age. Hand-washing technique is especially important during toilet training. After each visit to the toilet, children should wash their hands with soap and warm water for at least 20 seconds, and make sure they rinse thoroughly. It will probably be a while before young children can successfully wash their hands on their own, so stay close by and supervise even those who insist on doing it 'on my own'. To make hand-washing more fun, you could sing a song or make it into a little game. Make sure there is always a step stool close by so that your child can reach the sink.

About pets

Dogs can pass on germs by licking a child's face or hands, so try to discourage this. Make sure children's hands are always washed after they have touched animals.

Make sure all children understand the importance of thorough hand-washing.

Boys' toilet tips

Little boys can benefit from some specific tips as they learn to use the toilet. If their dad, or an older brother, can show them what to do, so much the better. If aiming their penis into the toilet to pee is proving tricky, small 'o' shaped cereal or squares of toilet paper can be put in the toilet to give boys something to aim at. Teach boys how to lift the toilet seat and lid before they pee and make sure both are secure, in case they fall down and hurt them. Encourage boys not to drip pee on the floor, or leave lots of splashes on the rim. Try to help them learn to use the toilet considerately from the start.

Using the toilet properly is a skill, like any other, that a child needs help to master.

For some children, getting out of, and back into, their clothes, is the trickiest part of a visit to the bathroom.

Older children may start having more accidents when a new baby arrives. This phase usually passes quickly.

Pride and praise

If your child visits the toilet and returns, dressed, with washed hands, you can congratulate yourself on having a child who is fully toilet-trained during the day. As always, where children are concerned, there may still be hiccups ahead, but focusing on positive things will encourage them, and help you deal with any setbacks.

Keep up the praise

Children thrive on praise, so, without over-doing things, remember to keep letting them know how proud you are of them using the toilet. Tell them that it's great for you not to have to change their diapers or empty potties anymore and that you really appreciate what they are doing.

Many children enjoy the chance to show others that they are now too grown-up for a potty by handing it over to a smaller child. They will probably be extremely proud of the fact that they don't need it any more.

Relapses

It's very common for children to have the occasional accident, even after months out of diapers during the day. There can be a variety of reasons why this happens: they could be sick, very absorbed in their play, or feeling nervous or unsure. One of the most common causes for relapses is a stressful event in a child's life, such as starting preschool, the arrival of a new brother or sister, going to the hospital or moving house.

If a child seems sick, or is experiencing pain when they pee or poop, take them to a doctor right away. If they seem well, but are just not getting to the toilet in time, try to be patient: offer reassurance, and wait for them to get back on track. If problems persist, you may have to consider going back to potties for a while, to reestablish some basic rules.

Problem solving

No childcare expert can guarantee that, even
if you follow a program or list of instructions
to the letter, a child will be potty or toilet-trained
at the end of them. Many people encounter setbacks
along the way. This part of the book looks at
specific problems parents often face, and
offers help in solving them.

What's going wrong?

How to help children who are slower
becoming potty-trained than others

Guidance for when children are reluctant to
poop anywhere other than in a diaper

Tips for tricky situations, such as a child having
frequent accidents at day care or when you are out

Advice on more serious problems, such as chronic
constipation or uncontrollable peeing

Common problems

On the next few pages, you'll find advice on solving the most common daytime potty-training problems. If you are very worried about your child's toileting behavior, always ask your child's doctor for help.

Q: Why won't my child 'get' the potty-training message?

A: Parents often get extremely anxious if they feel that their child is taking longer to potty-train than others. This book emphasizes throughout how important it is that you stay positive, and don't put pressure on your child. Your getting stressed about it all will probably only delay toilet-training even further. Hard as it may be, some children just take longer than others. Follow the guidance in this book and be assured that your child will be clean and dry in the end.

Q: My child will not wipe her own bottom. When should I make her?

A: You'll do a much better job of this than most small children, so it's tempting to keep doing it, rather than letting them try. It is very important that a child's bottom is as clean as possible, to avoid soreness, germs and unpleasant smells. It's best to give them lots of practice in learning how to wipe their bottoms (before bathtime is a good time), but check how they have done until they are at least five years old. Once your child starts school, teachers won't have time to help them, so aim for them to be accomplished bottom-wipers by then.

Q: Why does my child keep pooping in his pants?

A: A few children soil their pants because they don't like using the potty or toilet, actively preferring to poop in their pants, but most do it because they are constipated. If they put off pooping (perhaps because of one painful experience), eventually, semi-liquid poop from behind the hard, more solid poop in their bowel leaks out into their underwear. Make sure your child's diet includes lots of fruit and vegetables and plenty of fluids, as this helps prevent constipation. If the problem persists, see a doctor.

Q: Why does my child wet her pants at day care, but not at home?

A: Many children have accidents when they're somewhere less familiar than home, and may need more frequent prompting to go to the bathroom if they're busy playing. Talk to your child and to the staff (without your child overhearing) about what's happening. Perhaps your child is upset at day care or dislikes the toilets? Keep sending dry clothes, don't get upset and keep praising potty successes at home.

Q: My 4 year-old was clean and dry, but now has lots of accidents, which is frustrating. What should I do?

A: Many children have relapses like this. The novelty of using the potty may have worn off. Talk to your child about what they should be doing, what they are doing and how uncomfortable wet clothes must be. Would they prefer only to use the toilet, or to move the potty somewhere else? If they want to go back into diapers, it may help to let them for a short time.

Q: Why will my child only poop in a diaper?

A: Some children go through a phase of not wanting to push a poop out into what feels like nothingness (i.e. the potty or toilet). We may find this difficult to understand, but it's vital to accept a child's worries and help them overcome them. Until this phase passes, placing toilet paper inside the bowl to stop the splash can help, as can putting the child on the toilet when they are more likely to need to poop, such as after a meal.

Children are quick to pick up on your anxiety if there are problems with toilet training, so stay calm and reassuring.

More problems

Q: I think my child is not using the potty deliberately. What can I do?

A: It's hard to know if a child is deliberately not getting to the toilet or potty in time. It may be that your child can see that their accidents get them attention from you, even if it is negative attention. Try not reacting to their accidents, but cleaning up without showing any emotion. If your child is old enough, getting them to help clean up (without getting upset) can work too. If they do use the potty, praise them and give them lots of positive attention whenever you can. This may help break the cycle.

Q: Now that he is wearing underwear, my son has started playing with his penis a lot. Should I worry?

A: Small children are naturally fascinated with parts of their bodies, and it's entirely normal for boys and girls to touch their genitals. The best approach is not to stop them, but to tell them not to touch these parts of their bodies in front of other people, as these parts of their bodies are private. Forbidding it altogether might make it seem all the more appealing.

Q: I am getting extremely annoyed with my child every time she has an accident. What can I do?

A: Most children get distressed if their caregiver is upset with them. If potty-training is making your relationship suffer, is it worth persevering? Think about taking a break from it, asking someone else to take over for a while or trying again another time when you feel more relaxed. There are also some tips to try on pages 26 and 27. You may both have gotten into a cycle of stress that you need to break, as it's probably making you both very miserable.

Q: My child will only use our toilet at home. This makes going out very difficult. What should I do?

A: This problem may have sprung from just one negative experience when using another toilet (such as finding it dirty), but it is exasperating. You could hold your child above 'other' toilet seats, so that they make no contact with them at all. Using a toilet yourself first may also allay their fears, as can wiping it thoroughly for them first. Try and keep your own negative reactions to dirty and unfamiliar toilets to a minimum.

Q: I've tried potty-training my 3 ½ year-old several times but we still have wet pants. What shall I do?

A: It might be worth canceling everything for a day or so and really focusing on training. As your child is old enough to go straight to the toilet, skip the potty and use the time to help them make the link between needing to use the toilet and getting to it in time. Praise any successes, and consider small prizes too. It could be a good opportunity to replace past negative attempts with an intensive, but positive, one.

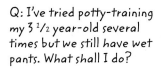

Q: My 3 year-old girl isn't interested in coming out of diapers at all and gets very upset if I suggest using the potty. What can I do?

A: It's good that you're still 'suggesting' rather than 'forcing' her to use the potty, as this is one thing you can't make a child do. By the age of three, your child should be capable of being potty-trained, but may, for a variety of reasons, have pitted her will against yours and decided not to try. Follow the advice and guidelines in this book, and trust that, eventually, your child will join other children successfully out of diapers. If you've still made no progress by the time your daughter is four, ask her doctor.

Q: My 4 year-old son can't pee standing up. Will he ever do it?

A: Yes, if only when he sees other boys doing it at day care, or at school, as he won't want to be different. If his dad, or an older brother can show your son how such things are done and let him have lots of practice himself, this will help. Otherwise, don't worry; he will learn in his own good time.

Asking for help

Sometimes a child may encounter problems such as those on this page, which need expert help to solve. If you are ever really worried about a child's toileting behavior, remember that health professionals are there to help you, and have a lot of experience and expertise in all areas of child development, so ask for their help if you need it.

Chronic constipation

Many small children are constipated from time to time, or produce hard poops that hurt their bottoms. Time, a balanced diet, and plenty of fluids usually sort this out. In some cases, and for a variety of reasons, children get so distressed about pooping that they refuse to go at all for fairly long periods of time. Unfortunately, however, as their body's need to poop increases, so does their fear.

This cycle can lead to enormous distress for the child and those caring for them, but it can be solved with expert help. Doctors often prescribe mild laxatives to soften things up: these may have to be taken for some time, to help the child go to the bathroom regularly and overcome their anxiety. Stay calm if your child is panicking about pooping, as your stress, plus their anxiety, will make their problem worse.

It's very important to make sure your child's diet always contains plenty of fresh fruit and vegetables.

Infections

If a child is experiencing unusual pain when they pee, or has cloudy pee, they may have an infection in their urinary tract. Girls are more prone to these. A course of antibiotics from their doctor will usually clear these infections up.

Wet underwear

Some children are regularly unable to control the flow of urine from their bladder in time to reach a potty or toilet. They may soak their clothes and the floor without a moment's notice. This is embarrassing for them, especially if they're at school, and you need expert support to tackle it. There are several solutions, from drawing a star on a child's hand as a reminder to go potty, to medication that can control the flow of urine in children over six years old. Talk to your doctor about which one will help your child. You'll find information about nighttime bed-wetting, called enuresis, in the next part of the book.

Dry nights

Most children are still wearing diapers at
night long after they are clean and dry
during the day. This part of the book
gives you some guidance in helping your
child learn how to be clean and dry
at night, as well.

Peaceful nights

How to know when your child is ready to come
out of diapers at night

Guidelines on getting your child, and their bed,
ready to try a diaperless night

Different tactics for overcoming any
setbacks you come across

Suggestions for dealing with the problem of
regular bedwetting in older children (known as enuresis)

Nights and diapers

As a general rule, most children are dry at night by their fourth birthday, but many continue to wear a diaper at night for longer. It takes time to gain enough control to hold it, or to get up and go to the potty or toilet, during the night.

The nighttime diaper can be hard to say goodbye to for some children, as it's very much a part of bedtime.

There's no rush to take off nighttime diapers. Nobody except your family will know if your child wears one.

Most young children spend at least 12 hours in bed each night. That's a long time for them to last without peeing, so their bladder needs to be mature enough to cope. There's absolutely no point taking off nighttime diapers unless you are fairly sure your child is ready to be without them. Some typical signs that they might be are on the left. Few children do all of these things, but if they do two of them, they may be ready to be diaperless at night.

Signs to spot

• Is your child waking up and telling you they need to potty?

• Is your child's nighttime diaper dry most mornings?

• Is your child reluctant to put on a diaper at night?

• Does your child pull their diaper off during the night?

Soggy morning diapers

Many children who are almost ready to be dry at night wake up with a soaking diaper. The bladder is at its fullest in the morning, so it's common for a child to pee a lot just before, or just as, they wake up. If this is happening to your child, you could wake them up a little earlier for a few days and take them to the potty to pee there instead. If this stops them from wetting their diaper, you can gradually make the wake-up time a little later each day.

Nighttime trips to the bathroom

When they first stop putting their children in diapers at night, some people decide to try to lessen the risk of being woken in the small hours by taking children to sit on the toilet at some point during the night. Some people wake their child to walk to the bathroom themselves, others pick them up gently and carry them there. Most take their child to the bathroom just before they go to bed themselves and many people continue to do this for several years, even when the child is less likely to have an accident during the night. Childcare experts are divided, however, on whether adopting this strategy is a good idea, so the decision about whether to do it is up to you.

It is not easy to carry a child to the bathroom without waking them up...

... or for a sleepy child to know what you want them to do.

Nighttime trips to the bathroom can save wet beds, and broken nights, for some families – certainly in the short term – but there are disadvantages. The main drawback is that the child is more asleep than awake throughout, so you are, in reality, encouraging them to pee in their sleep. Carrying a child to the bathroom will also disturb their sleep to some degree, and you may actually wake them right up. Weigh the pros and cons carefully before you decide if this strategy will work for you.

Children often sleep very deeply, and may not wake at all when you carry them at night.

The final diaper

The last diaper your child ever wears will probably be their nighttime diaper. These pages guide you through putting your child to bed without a diaper for the first time. If you are prepared, and your child wants to try going to bed without a diaper, they are much more likely to wake up in a dry bed. Don't expect miracles, though: there may well be a few accidents.

Bedtime preparations

On the left, you can read the steps you need to follow on the night you decide not to put a diaper on your child. Before you begin, explain that your child is a big boy or girl now, and doesn't need to wear a diaper anymore. This won't guarantee success, but it's better to involve them from the start. Some people put a potty near their child's bed, in case they do need to go to the bathroom in the night. Leaving a dim night-light on in their bedroom makes it easier for a child to find the potty. It also makes it less disruptive for you to go in and change wet bedding, should you need to.

Be prepared

1. Put a waterproof mattress cover onto your child's crib or bed, under the sheet. They are easily sponged dry (unlike a wet mattress).

2. Have plenty of dry bedding and pajamas on hand. Fumbling for them in the middle of the night will mean less sleep for both of you.

3. Don't worry about letting your child have a small drink near bedtime, but make sure they use the bathroom before they get into bed.

4. In the morning, take your child to the toilet as soon as they wake up. If their bed is dry, give them plenty of praise. If not, try again.

It will take time for a child to recognize the signs of needing to pee or poop when they are fast asleep.

Not a good time

Few people are at their best when they are woken from a deep sleep to change wet sheets and pajamas. Even fewer are gracious if this has happened several times. Many children will wake up, and wake you up, when they feel their bed is wet, whereas others will sleep on until morning, untroubled. Try to keep things calm and dimly-lit as you do what needs doing. Changing wet beds in the middle of the night is not the best part of parenting, but it won't last forever.

Your child will probably be upset about having had an accident, will not like waking up in a cold, damp bed and will certainly not have wet themselves deliberately. If accidents persist, see page 52 for more information about regular bedwetting, or enuresis.

Try not to be too grumpy when your child wakes you up in the night.

Nights away

Children who have been diaperless at night for several months often have relapses when they are troubled about something, or when they are in an unfamiliar environment, such as someone else's house, and bed. If you're going to be away from home soon after a child has come out of nighttime diapers, consider taking your own bedding including the waterproof mattress cover. You could also put extra padding, such as towels, under your child at night. If you are staying with other people, it's probably best to explain your child's situation when you arrive, as nobody will want you to worry.

Useful tip
Disposable diaper pads, that protect mattresses, are very useful for trips away from home.

Wet beds

Studies show that a surprising number of children wet their bed on a regular basis, so don't feel you are unusual, or alone, if your child is doing so. Regular bedwetting, or enuresis, can be distressing and disruptive for the whole family, but there are ways of dealing with it. This page offers you some help and advice.

When to worry

Experts usually don't consider bedwetting to be a problem until a child is over five years old, and most doctors will not suggest getting specialist help until after this age. There are various treatments available, (depending on why the child is wetting the bed) and most are successful.

If bedwetting is really troubling a young child, or affecting their self-confidence, consider asking for help earlier. Your child's doctor or nurse may have some straightforward suggestions as to why your child is peeing while asleep. For instance, a small reward for each dry night can help, as some children simply don't feel like getting out of their warm bed at night to visit the toilet.

The last thing you want to do is to make any child anxious about wetting their bed as that can increase the likelihood of them doing it for longer. As long as it's sorted out before they need to sleep away from home for a sleepover at a friend's house, for example, don't let it become a major source of anxiety for anyone.

Boys and bedwetting

Research shows that little boys are more prone to bedwetting than girls, and that it seems to take them longer to gain enough bladder control not to need to pee during the night. Knowing this may help you stay patient as you change their wet bedding yet again.

Useful tip
If your child wets the bed regularly, have dry clothes and bedding ready, to make changing them as quick and calm as you can.

Boys mature more slowly than girls in several ways throughout childhood, and there's nothing you can do to change that fact.

Useful information

This, final, part of the book has information that you may find helpful as you potty-train a child. Some of the material here expands on subjects looked at on earlier pages, and some of it is new.

What will I find?

A step-by-step guide on how to potty-train, bringing together all the main points made in this book

Information about different approaches to training

General information about children with special needs, and suggestions as to how to use the internet as a support

A list of simple mistakes it's all too easy to make when potty-training a child (to help you not to make them)

One step at a time

This book emphasizes throughout that there is no single program of potty-training that will guarantee success for every child. Each child is different and so are his or her family circumstances. However, it may be helpful to have the overall approach that this book suggests broken down into a series of easy-to-follow steps, so this is what you will find on the following pages.

You don't need to follow these steps rigidly: few children will allow you to, anyway. They are designed as a framework, a useful reference, as you train your child. You may find you miss some steps completely, or do some in a different order. Every parent will work out their own ways of overcoming problems, and arriving at their goal: a happy, diaperless child. As you look through the steps, keep in mind that there may be several months between some stages, depending on how old, and mature, your child is.

Learning to use the potty is one of the many, many things your child has to learn.

Useful tip

Trust your instincts. Remember that you know your child better than anyone else does.

Things to remember

As you read the steps on the following pages, keep these three things in mind.

• Expect and accept setbacks and accidents. Potty-training is a learning process.

• Don't impose a training schedule that suits you, on your child. It's pointless.

• Make sure that your child understands what you want them to do, and be consistent.

Potty-training: start to finish

1

Experts don't recommend even trying to start training a child until they are between 24 and 30 months old. Some children are mature enough to be trained by the age of two, but most are not.

2

Buy a potty (or several, if you wish) and talk to your child about what they are for. Explain that big girls and boys pee and poop in them and that they will too.

3

Let your child become familiar with the potty and try sitting on it (in or out of a diaper). Don't let them play with it too much, though. It's not a toy.

4

When your child comes to the bathroom with you, talk to them about what happens there. Choose, and use, the 'toilet words' you want them to say, with care. Children will repeat what they hear.

5

Encourage your child to tell you when they have peed or pooped in their diaper. They usually learn this before they learn when they are going to go.

6

If your child is willing, take their diaper off for a while. Get them to sit on the potty for a few minutes at a regular time each day, such as after a meal or before bed.

7

Look at children's books, and watch DVDs about potties, to help a child see what they are for and that they are a part of all kinds of children's lives.

Don't deny your child a drink if they need one.

8

Gradually increase the number of times your child sits on the potty. Make sure they drink plenty of fluids, so that they need to pee regularly.

9

Build up diaper-free time at home, making sure your child understands you would like them to pee and poop in the potty now. Praise any successes they have, but don't expect too much of them.

10

Make a special shopping trip together to choose some new underwear for your child. Remember to buy quite a few pairs so you don't have to do laundry too often.

11

When your child seems ready, it's time to get rid of diapers. Explain what's going to happen and tell your child to tell you whenever they need the potty.

Children need to be reminded to sit on the potty if they are very involved in their play.

12

Remind them fairly frequently to use the potty, but don't interrupt their play too often. Your goal is for them to learn to know when they need to go for themselves.

13

Keep praising all successes in the potty, and try to deal with accidents calmly. Remember that your child is learning lots of new skills at once.

14

When you go out, either put your child in a diaper, training pants, or put them on the potty just before you leave and go prepared to deal with any accidents. Most children will have a few.

15

You will need to wipe your child's bottom and supervise hand-washing for quite a while. Show them good hygiene habits until they can put them into practice for themselves later.

16

If all is going well, encourage your child to find the potty themselves when they need to go by reducing the frequency of your reminders. Consider offering a small reward for successful potty use.

17

If things are not going well, think about stopping training for a while. Don't risk making your child upset or fearful about the whole business. Many children need several attempts.

18

If your child is interested in using the toilet, a plastic child's toilet seat will fit their bottom better. A plastic step makes getting on and off the toilet easier for a small child.

19

Gradually, help children learn to wipe their bottom, flush the toilet, wash their hands and pull their underwear, pants or tights back up on their own. Check how they cope until you are confident they can manage.

20

If you are worried about any aspect of potty-training, or your child's behavior and toileting needs, always ask their doctor for advice.

When your child stops wearing a diaper at night, they are fully toilet-trained.

21

Try to lose nighttime diapers when your child's diapers are dry each morning, when they aren't happy wearing a diaper, or they get up to pee. Protect their mattress before you put them to bed diaperless.

Other approaches

This book suggests one approach to potty-training your child, but there are other methods out there, such as those discussed earlier in the book. Here is more detail about some of the other methods used to train babies and toddlers.

Starting early

In some parts of the world, especially in warm climates, babies don't wear diapers at all; they are held over a potty from birth. For this approach to work, parents need to learn to spot a baby's bodily signals, and predict when they need to go to the bathroom in time to hold them over a potty. In developed countries, experts do not recommend this method of training, and it is unusual for parents to try it, but, for some people, it feels right. Here's how the method works.

It is vital to have a very good understanding of your child's needs and behavior for the baby training method to work.

Signs and sounds

1. Parents study their baby's toileting habits closely, getting to know if they pee and poop at certain times, and interpreting signs that they need to go.

2. After some time, parents should, ideally, begin to know when it is the right time to hold their child over a potty by being 'in tune' with their child.

3. Some parents make a specific noise to encourage their baby to go to the bathroom. Ideally, when the baby hears that sound, they will pee or poop.

4. Slightly older babies can learn to make certain signs or gestures that mean they need to use the potty. This takes time, and plenty of practice.

Useful tip

Talk to other parents about how they trained their children, and which techniques they would recommend.

This method is better for the environment, as no diapers are used, but it requires an enormous commitment from parents. The time they invest may increase the emotional bond between them and their baby, but for a long while, the child will rely largely on the adult to know that they need to pee or poop, rather than understanding their needs themselves. Relapses are common, as are other toileting problems, with this method.

Intensive training

Some parents choose a date, take their child's daytime diapers off and stay at home until the child uses the potty. If you have time, and can suspend normal life for a while, this method may suit you. The steps to follow are on the right. This method only works if you try it at the right time for your child. If you do, it may well work, but, if not, you will both have a miserable, negative, few days and probably have to give up and face doing it all again. Only attempt this method if you feel your child is already showing signs of being ready to be trained (see page 20).

No one can force a child to use the potty. It's best if they are willing, and ready, to do so.

Intensive method

1. Buy a supply of underwear and comfortable clothing for your child. Cancel everything for the next few days. Get cleaning supplies ready.

2. Explain what will happen, then take your child's diaper off. Take them to sit on the potty very regularly, for several minutes at a time.

3. Make sure your child drinks plenty of fluids, such as diluted fruit juice, to make them need to pee often. Keep putting them on the potty.

4. Keep reinforcing the message that your child needs to pee and poop in the potty. Praise successes and deal with accidents calmly.

Child-centered training

Many experts suggest waiting for a child to indicate that they want to use the potty or toilet rather than diapers and then helping them make the transition into underwear. Research shows that children today are being trained later, and bigger, more absorbent, diapers make it easier to keep a child in diapers for longer. In fact, some diapers are so efficient that children may not feel uncomfortable in a wet or dirty diaper and therefore may not learn to understand their body's signals. If your child is showing signs of being ready to be potty-trained, don't ignore them. It's vital to try to balance your needs and your child's needs.

It can be embarrassing for a child to be in diapers longer than any of their playmates.

Special needs

Potty-training children with special needs is, in many cases, just like training any other child. There is no guaranteed method, each child makes different demands, and you need plenty of patience. There is also a huge range of different needs included in the term 'special needs', as parents will be aware. This page gives a very basic overview of things that might be helpful.

Getting advice

It is a good idea to talk to your child's doctor or therapist about any specific concerns you may have about potty-training before you begin. Some children with particular needs will learn to understand and control their body's toileting behavior with ease, whereas others will take longer and need more help from their parents and caregivers.

Professionals are trained to advise on this. There are also books and websites with detailed information about particular special needs. You will find a list of them on the Usborne Quicklinks Website (see opposite page). On the left are three things it might be helpful for you to bear in mind before you begin potty-training a child with special needs.

Don't hesitate to ask for professional help if you need it.

Three tips

• Try to focus not on your child's age in months and years, but on their physical and emotional readiness to be trained.

• Look for the signs of readiness to start being trained listed on page 20. Your child must be ready to come out of diapers to master the toileting skills they need next.

• Remember that your child not only has to understand what their body needs to do, but also be able to get to (or show that they want to get to) the potty or toilet in time to do it.

Some children take longer than others to learn what a potty is for.

What not to do

Potty-training a small child is not always easy and parents often make common mistakes. On the right are three of the most common. If you do them too, you are not alone, but be aware that they will only make a bad situation worse.

It's not always easy to stay cheerful during potty-training, but try not to let it spoil the time you spend with your child.

Three mistakes

1. Many parents try to potty-train their children too soon, before they are ready, because it suits them to do so.

2. A lot of people feel pressured by others to potty-train their child before they feel they want to.

3. Lack of consistency can confuse children. If you don't want your child to use a diaper, avoid letting them do so after you've made the switch.

Internet links

The internet is a good source of information for parents and caregivers. At the Usborne Quicklinks Website there are links to lots of websites you may find useful and other things you can download. To visit the sites, go to **www.usborne-quicklinks.com** and type the keywords 'potty training'. Here are some of the things you can do via Usborne Quicklinks:

• Print out the potty training chart from pages 55 to 57 of this book.

• Download reward charts and achievement certificates to help motivate your toddler.

• Watch video clips with lots of extra advice and tips on potty training your child.

• Print out coloring pages and song sheets to help make potty training a positive experience.

There is a huge amount of advice about potty-training on the internet (but only some of it may be useful).

Internet safety

The websites recommended in Usborne Quicklinks are regularly reviewed. However the content of a website may change at any time and Usborne Publishing is not responsible for the content or availability of websites other than its own.

Index

With thanks to...

Bethan, Rhiannon and Mari;
Staff, parents and children at Cannons Health Club Nursery, Surbiton,
and Finley Mason;
Sam Taplin for proofreading;
Jessica Greenwell for indexing and website research;
Claire Masset for additional picture research.

Photo credits:

The publishers are grateful to the following for permission to reproduce material:

p9 © Luca DiCecco/Alamy; p15 © Bubbles Photolibrary/Alamy;
p18 © Jose Luis Pelaez, Inc./Corbis; p21 © Steve Prezant/Corbis;
p49 © Digital Vision/Alamy; p50 © Peter Dazeley/Alamy;
p54 © Picture Partners/Alamy

Additional illustrations: Dubravka Kolanovic
Digital imaging: Keith Furnival
Americanization: Carrie Armstrong and Jessica Greenwell

Every effort has been made to trace and acknowledge ownership of copyright. If any rights have been
omitted, the publishers offer to rectify this in any subsequent editions following notification.